SO BIG
Compared to What?

FREAKY-STRANGE
Buildings

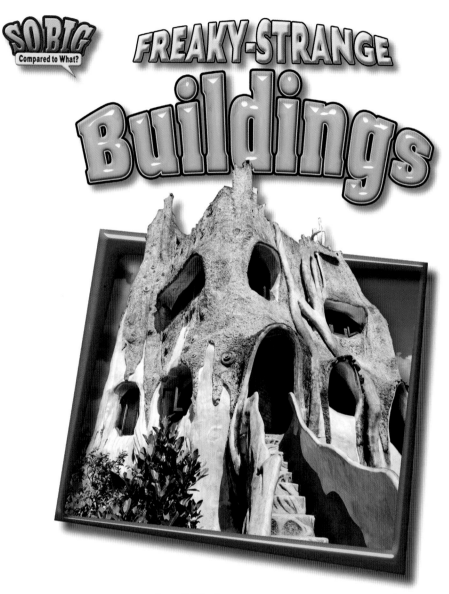

by Michael Sandler

Consultant: Paul F. Johnston, Ph.D.
Washington, D.C.

BEARPORT
PUBLISHING

New York, New York

Credits

Cover and Title Page, © Imagebroker/SuperStock; TOC, © Yinghua/Dreamstime; 4, © Imagebroker/SuperStock; 5L, © Piotr J. Walczak Photography; 5R, © Allstar Picture Library/Alamy; 6, © Prisma/SuperStock; 7L, © Yejun/Dreamstime; 7R, © IndexStock/SuperStock; 8, © Randall Hyman Photography; 9T, © Randall Hyman Photography; 9B, © Jonathan Moreau; 10, © Bernhard Spöttel/Red Bull Content Pool; 11L, © Sven Rosenhall/Nordicphotos/Alamy; 11R, © Arcaid/Robert Harding World Imagery/Getty Images; 12L, © Jesus Diges/AFP/Getty Images; 12R, © JTB Photo/SuperStock; 13, © Travel Library Limited/SuperStock; 14, © Minden Pictures/SuperStock; 15T, © Ian Nellist/Alamy; 15B, © ColsTravel/Alamy; 16, © Jochen Tack/Alamy; 17, © Jean-Pierre Lescourret/SuperStock; 18, © CB2/ZOB WENN Photos/Newscom; 19, © David R. Frazier Photolibrary, Inc./Alamy; 20, © Axiom Photographic Limited/SuperStock; 21, © Charles Bowman/Alamy; 22A, © George Sheldon/Alamy; 22B, © Renatas Duda; 22C, © Janusz Gniadek/Alamy; 22D, © Imagebroker/SuperStock.

Publisher: Kenn Goin
Senior Editor: Lisa Wiseman
Creative Director: Spencer Brinker
Photo Researcher: Picture Perfect Professionals, LLC

Library of Congress Cataloging-in-Publication Data

Sandler, Michael, 1965-
  Freaky-strange buildings / by Michael Sandler ; consultant, Paul F. Johnston.
      p. cm. — (So big compared to what?)
  Includes bibliographical references and index.
  ISBN-13: 978-1-61772-305-6 (library binding)
  ISBN-10: 1-61772-305-3 (library binding)
  1. Buildings—Miscellanea. I. Johnston, Paul F. II. Title.
  TH149.S26 2012
  720—dc22

2011014175

For more information, write to Bearport Publishing Company, Inc.,
45 West 21st Street, Suite 3B, New York, New York 10010.
Printed in the United States of America in North Mankato, Minnesota.

072011
042711CGF

10 9 8 7 6 5 4 3 2 1

CONTENTS

Freaky-Strange Buildings 4

Oriental Pearl TV Tower 6

The Community Bookshelf 8

Turning Torso 10

The Sagrada Família 12

The Hotel Luna Salada 14

Burj Al Arab Hotel 16

The Longaberger Home Office 18

The Guggenheim Museum Bilbao 20

More Freaky-Strange Buildings 22

Glossary 23

Index 24

Bibliography 24

Read More 24

Learn More Online 24

About the Author 24

FREAKY-STRANGE BUILDINGS

Chefs come up with crazy meals. Fashion designers create wacky outfits. Automakers build cars that look both wild and weird. Why should **architects** be any different? Sometimes they design buildings that are just plain strange. The results make people stop and stare.

It looks more like a cave than a building, but Crazy House in Dalat, Vietnam, is actually a hotel.

In this book, you will take a tour of some of the world's strangest-looking buildings. Some are made to look like ordinary household objects. Others are constructed from very unusual materials. All of them, however, are unlike the homes, offices, and hotels you usually see every day. These buildings aren't just strange—they're freaky strange!

At 272 feet (83 m), the 20-story Robot Building is more than 80 times taller than R2-D2, the famous robot from the *Star Wars* movie series.

R2-D2

The Robot Building in Bangkok, Thailand, was built to look like. . . a robot! The architect got the idea from looking at his son's toy robot.

ORIENTAL PEARL TV TOWER

Opened: 1994 **Where:** Shanghai, China **Height:** 1,535 feet (468 m)

Freaky-Strange Feature: Eleven giant "pearls"

In the past 20 years, plenty of new buildings have been built in fast-growing Shanghai—China's largest city. Many are odd, but none are as **unique** as the Oriental Pearl TV Tower. A huge **tripod** base and eleven ball-shaped "pearls" give the tower its wild appearance—half amusement-park ride and half shish-kebab skewer. The different-sized pearls are a symbol of the city, once known as the Pearl of the **Orient**.

The tower's main purpose is broadcasting radio and television signals, but it's also a sightseeing attraction. Visitors ride to an observation deck in the upper pearl using speedy elevators that move upward at 23 feet per second (7 mps). They are so fast that if the elevators were used to transport people from the base of Mount Everest to its peak—a distance of nearly 5.5 miles (8.8 km)—it would take less than half an hour.

The big upper pearl holds a **revolving** restaurant and a disco. This pearl is almost 150 feet (46 m) in diameter— more than 6,000 times bigger than an average-size pearl on a necklace.

The Oriental Pearl is the fifth-tallest TV tower in the world and was the tallest structure in China until 2007. At 1,535 feet (468 m), it's about five times taller than the Statue of Liberty.

The tower's five small middle pearls make up a 20-**suite** hotel. At 755 feet (230 m) above the ground, some of the upper rooms are even higher than the top of Saint Louis's Gateway Arch.

The Gateway Arch in St. Louis, Missouri

THE COMMUNITY BOOKSHELF

Opened: 2004   **Where:** Kansas City, Missouri   **Size:** 152,864 square feet (14,201 sq m)

Freaky-Strange Feature: Wall of books

When people walk down Tenth Street in Kansas City, Missouri, they often stop and stare at the public library's parking garage. Instead of an ordinary concrete wall, there appears to be a huge bookshelf, filled with oversized books.

Though the books look real, they're not. They're made of plastic. The Community Bookshelf, as it's called, makes up the parking garage's south wall. The books were chosen from suggestions made by Kansas City residents. Some are about the city's history. Others are classics, such as *The Lord of the Rings* and *Charlotte's Web*. One is a group of children's favorites, including *Winnie-the-Pooh*, *The Wonderful Wizard of Oz*, and *Green Eggs and Ham*.

A staircase to the garage

Bookends at each end of the shelf appear to hold the books in place. In fact, the bookends contain elevators and stairs that library patrons can take to get to their cars. There are also staircases to the garage that look like books lying flat on their sides.

A five-story parking garage is located behind the books. With over 150,000 square feet (13,935 sq m)—about the size of nine ice hockey rinks—there's enough space for almost 500 cars.

At 25 feet (8 m) tall, each book in the bookshelf is about as tall as 300 average-size paperback books stacked on top of each other.

TURNING TORSO

Opened: 2005   **Where:** Malmö, Sweden   **Height:** 623 feet (190 m)
Freaky-Strange Feature: The building's 90-degree twist

Turning Torso in Malmö, Sweden, was built with a real twist. The architect, Santiago Calatrava, wanted the building to **invoke** the motion of a human body turning upward. To do so, the building twists from bottom to top, 90 degrees clockwise—a full quarter turn. The side of the building that faces east at ground level, for example, faces south by the top of the building.

The twisting tower is all the more impressive because of its size. At 623 feet (190 m), it's the tallest apartment building in the **European Union** and **Scandinavia**'s tallest skyscraper. It has over 145 apartments and about 290,626 square feet (27,000 sq m) of floor space. That's nearly six times as much floor space as there is in the White House.

In August 2006, Turning Torso was the site of a daring parachute and **BASE jump.** First, skydiver Felix Baumgartner hopped out of a helicopter and parachuted onto the building's roof. Then, using a second parachute, he hopped off the roof and floated safely to the ground.

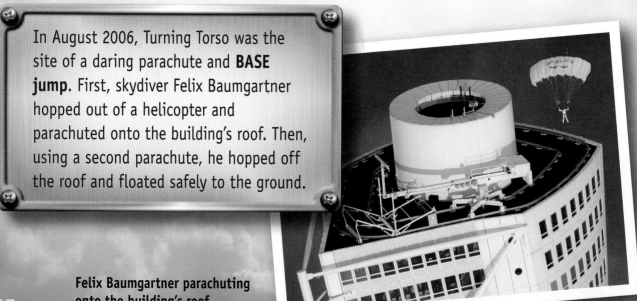

Felix Baumgartner parachuting onto the building's roof

Turning Torso is made up of nine **pentagon**-shaped sections stacked on top of each other. Each section is about as tall as a five-story apartment building.

Three high-speed elevators take residents to their apartments in Turning Torso at 16.5 feet per second (5 mps). It takes just 38 seconds to go from the ground floor to the top of the building.

THE SAGRADA FAMÍLIA

Construction Began: 1882   **Where:** Barcelona, Spain   **Height:** 558 feet (170 m) when finished

Freaky-Strange Feature: The building's unique construction

Spanish architect Antonio Gaudí is famous for the many **innovative** buildings he built in Barcelona, Spain. The church he designed, the Sagrada Família, is probably his most extraordinary.

Columns that support the church's ceilings look like trees because Gaudí wanted the inside to feel like a forest. Twenty-two different kinds of stone have been used for the walls, handrails, staircases, and other building features. They add an unusual mix of texture and color to the building.

Adding to the uniqueness of the church are sculptures of seashells and fruit, as well as cave-like **recesses** that seem to drip with **stalactites**. Gaudí's unique design draws flocks of tourists—about 2.5 million visitors each year, more people than there are in the entire population of Houston, Texas.

The columns inside the church (left) were built to look like real trees (right).

Ten of the Sagrada Família's 18 towers are yet to be built. When finished, the central tower will have the tallest church **spire** in the world at 558 feet (170 m). That would be as tall as about 30 giraffes stacked on top of each other.

As of 2011, the church has been under construction for 129 years. That's more than 100 times as long as it took to complete the Empire State Building in New York City.

The church was unfinished when Gaudí died in 1926. However, work on the church continues today. The Sagrada Família is expected to be completed by 2026.

THE HOTEL LUNA SALADA

Opened: 2005   **Where:** Uyuni, Bolivia   **Size:** 21,528 square feet (2,000 sq m)

Freaky-Strange Feature: All-salt construction

Few places on Earth are stranger than Salar de Uyuni. Located in Bolivia, a country in South America, Salar de Uyuni is an enormous white **salt flat**—the leftovers of a giant **prehistoric** lake. Dotted with prickly cacti and pink flamingos where water remains, the Salar is home to the world's largest salt deposits.

It's also home to one of the world's strangest buildings—a hotel made almost entirely of salt. At the Hotel Luna Salada, the walls and ceilings are not the only things built out of salt—tables, beds, benches, chairs, and other furniture are as well!

The Luna Salada was constructed using over 200,000 salt blocks cut from the surface of the Salar de Uyuni. Scientists think there may be ten billion tons (9,071,847,400 metric tons) of salt in the ancient lake. In some areas, the salt is over 20 feet (6 m) deep.

At just over 4,000 square miles (10,360 sq km), the salt flat covers an area almost ten times bigger than the entire city of Los Angeles, California! It's so big that U.S. astronaut Neil Armstrong saw it from the moon!

The hotel is very comfortable, with soft mattresses, which are not made from salt, on the beds. However, visitors must get used to the **altitude.** At around 12,000 feet (3,658 m) above sea level, the hotel is about twice as high above sea level as Denver, Colorado, which is called the Mile–High City.

Hotel furniture made from salt

The Salar de Uyuni also contains the world's largest supply of lithium. This mineral is used in making batteries for electric cars, cell phones, and iPods.

BURJ AL ARAB HOTEL

Opened: 1999   **Where:** Dubai, United Arab Emirates   **Height:** 1,053 feet (321 m)

Freaky-Strange Feature: Giant sail shape

Dubai (duh-BYE) is a city in the United Arab Emirates, a country in the Middle East. It's home to many unique buildings, including the Burj Al Arab Hotel. This hotel is not only one of the tallest in the world, it's also among the most unusual. It sits on a man-made island and it was built to look like the sail of a dhow (DOU), an Arabic boat.

Of course, no dhow has ever had such an enormous sail. At 1,053 feet (321 m), the hotel is taller than most U.S. buildings, except for some skyscrapers found in Chicago and New York. Guests of the hotel stay in suites that span two floors. The biggest, which has its own movie theater, is 8,396 square feet (780 sq m)—over three times the size of an average American house.

The sea-themed hotel even has an underwater-style restaurant. To get to it, diners take a three-minute **simulated** submarine ride from the hotel lobby. Once seated in the restaurant, people can dine while watching sharks and other fish swim by in a giant rounded **aquarium** built into the wall.

The restaurant's aquarium holds about 260,000 gallons (984,207 l) of seawater. If the water was milk, it could serve four million kids at lunch!

What's the disk at the top of the tower used for? It's a landing pad for helicopters—the way many guests arrive at the hotel.

The steel used to build the Burj Al Arab Hotel weighed almost 10,000 tons (9,072 metric tons). That's about as much as 2,000 hippopotamuses weigh!

THE LONGABERGER HOME OFFICE

Opened: 1997   **Where:** Newark, Ohio   **Size:** 180,000 square feet (16,723 sq m)

Freaky-Strange Feature: Basket design

When it came time to build a new **headquarters** for the Longaberger Company, the company's chairman, David Longaberger, stunned the designers. He placed a basket down in front of them and said, "This is what I want."

David Longaberger got his wish. Today, the company's headquarters is a giant basket-shaped building. It looks exactly like the baskets the company makes, just bigger. In fact, at 208 feet (63 m) long by 142 feet (43 m) wide at the roof, it's 160 times bigger than a Longaberger Medium Market Basket.

A Longaberger Medium Market Basket

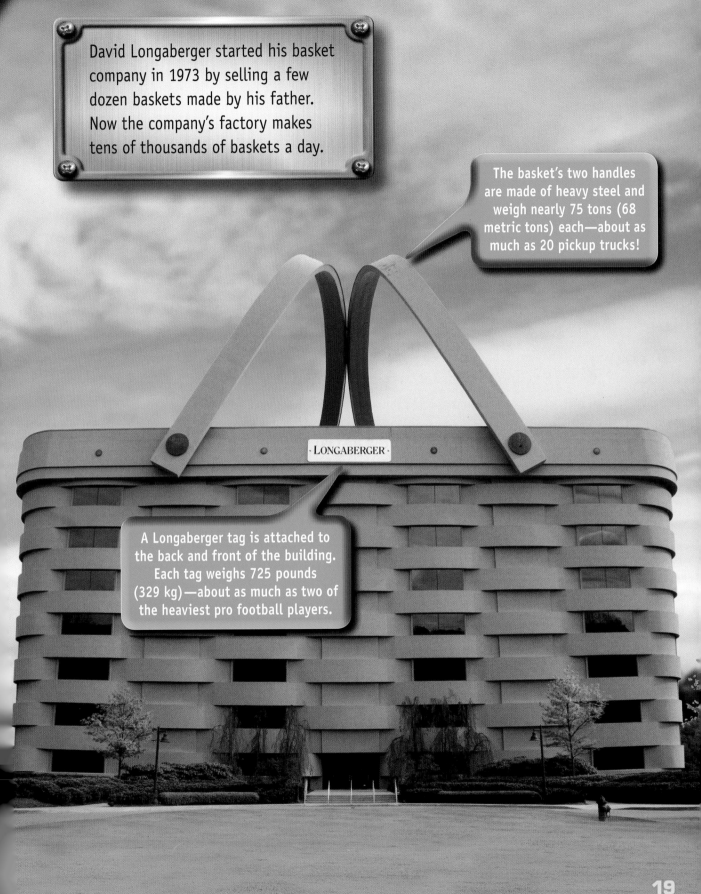

David Longaberger started his basket company in 1973 by selling a few dozen baskets made by his father. Now the company's factory makes tens of thousands of baskets a day.

The basket's two handles are made of heavy steel and weigh nearly 75 tons (68 metric tons) each—about as much as 20 pickup trucks!

LONGABERGER

A Longaberger tag is attached to the back and front of the building. Each tag weighs 725 pounds (329 kg)—about as much as two of the heaviest pro football players.

THE GUGGENHEIM MUSEUM BILBAO

Opened: 1997   **Where:** Bilbao, Spain   **Size:** 265,000 square feet (24,619 sq m)

Freaky-Strange Feature: Shiny, wave-like metal walls

In the early 1990s, the city of Bilbao was going through tough times. Factories had closed. Jobs were hard to find. As part of a plan to **renew** the city, planners built one of the wildest-looking art museums ever—the Guggenheim Museum Bilbao.

Architect Frank Gehry's museum looks like different things to different people. To some, it **resembles** a bucket of squirming fish. To others, it looks like a crazy ocean ship built from different materials such as **sandstone**, **titanium**, and glass.

No matter what people think it looks like, the massive building has plenty of room to show off pictures and sculptures. Its biggest gallery is 426 feet (130 m) long by 98 feet (30 m) wide—that's large enough to fit an entire soccer field inside.

The museum has over 118,000 square feet (10,963 sq m) of **exhibition space.** That's twice as much space as in an average American supermarket!

The titanium skin is incredibly thin at less than one–fiftieth of an inch (.5 mm) thick—even thinner than a person's eyelid skin.

One of the museum's most interesting features is its titanium skin. The skin sparkles in the sunlight and gives the Guggenheim a shimmering metallic look.

MORE FREAKY-STRANGE BUILDINGS

The Haines Shoe House, Pennsylvania

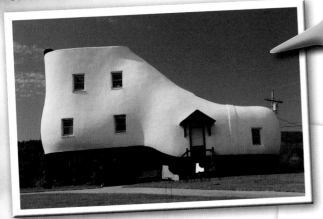

A little old woman could live in this shoe house and have plenty of space. At 48 feet (15 m) long, this house is about 50 times longer than an average-size man's boot.

Banknote Building, Lithuania

This office building was made to look like a banknote, an old Lithuanian paper bill from the 1920s. The building's surface is made of 4,500 pieces of glass that fit together like a jigsaw puzzle.

The Upside-Down House, Poland

This simple house would have taken just three weeks to build if it had been built right-side up. However, because workers felt dizzy and seasick while constructing the inside of the upside-down structure, it took 114 days to build—more than five times as long as it normally takes to build a simple house.

The Atomium, Belgium

Belgium's Atomium connects nine steel **spheres** and is built to resemble a **molecule** of iron. At 335 feet (102 m), it's much bigger than an iron molecule, however—about 165 billion times larger!

GLOSSARY

altitude (AL-ti-tood) the height of something above sea level

aquarium (uh-KWAIR-ee-uhm) large tanks or pools where different kinds of water animals and plants are kept

architects (AR-ki-tekts) people who design buildings and make sure they are built properly

BASE jump (BAYSS JUHMP) an activity in which people use parachutes to jump from cliffs or buildings

columns (KOL-uhmz) tall upright pillars that help support a building

European Union (*yu*-ruh-PEE-uhn YOON-yuhn) an organization of countries in Europe

exhibition space (*ek*-suh-BISH-uhn SPAYSS) the parts of a building, such as a museum, used to display paintings and other works of art

headquarters (HED-*kwor*-turz) the main office of a business or organization; the place where important decisions are made

innovative (in-uh-VAY-tiv) having new ideas about how something can be done

invoke (in-VOHK) to create an image of; to make a person think about

molecule (MOL-uh-kyool) the smallest part of a substance that can exist

Orient (OR-ee-uhnt) the countries of East Asia

pentagon (PEN-tuh-gon) a five-sided shape

prehistoric (*pree*-hi-STOR-ik) before the time when people began to use writing to record history

recesses (REE-sess-iz) spaces set back into a wall, often used for shelves

renew (ri-NOO) to make new again; to refresh

resembles (ri-ZEM-buhlz) looks like

revolving (ri-VOLV-ing) turning in a circle

salt flat (SAWLT FLAT) a flat area covered in salt that is left after a saltwater lake evaporates

sandstone (SAND-*stohn*) a type of rock

Scandinavia (skan-*duh*-NAY-vee-uh) a group of countries in Europe that includes Norway, Sweden, and Denmark

simulated (SIM-yuh-*lay*-tid) made to look real

spheres (SFIHRZ) ball-shaped objects

spire (SPIRE) a tall pointy structure on the top of a tower

stalactites (stuh-LAK-*tites*) cone-shaped mineral deposits that hang from the roof of a cave

suite (SWEET) a group of rooms that are connected

titanium (tye-TAY-nee-uhm) a light, strong metallic element

tripod (TRYE-*pod*) a stand or structure with three legs

unique (yoo-NEEK) one of a kind; like no other

INDEX

Atomium, The 22
Bangkok, Thailand 5
Banknote Building 22
Barcelona, Spain 12
Belgium 22
Bilbao, Spain 20
Burj Al Arab Hotel 16–17
Community Bookshelf, The 8–9
Crazy House 4
Dalat, Vietnam 4

Dubai, United Arab Emirates 16
Guggenheim Museum Bilbao 20–21
Haines Shoe House, The 22
Hotel Luna Salada, The 14–15
Kansas City, Missouri 8
Lithuania 22
Longaberger Home Office, The 18–19
Malmö, Sweden 10
Newark, Ohio 18

Oriental Pearl TV Tower 6–7
Pennsylvania 22
Poland 22
Robot Building 5
Sagrada Família, The 12–13
Shanghai, China 6–7
Turning Torso 10–11
Upside-Down House, The 22
Uyuni, Bolivia 14

BIBLIOGRAPHY

Wright, Lawrence. "Lithium Dreams." *The New Yorker* (March 22, 2010).

www.guggenheim.org

www.longaberger.com

READ MORE

DiPiazza, Francesca Davis. *Bolivia in Pictures.* Minneapolis, MN: Twenty-First Century Books (2008).

Rodriguez, Rachel Victoria. *Building on Nature: The Life of Antoni Gaudí.* New York: Henry Holt (2009).

LEARN MORE ONLINE

To learn more about freaky-strange buildings, visit
www.bearportpublishing.com/SoBigComparedtoWhat

ABOUT THE AUTHOR

Brooklyn-based writer Michael Sandler has written numerous books for kids and teens.